party plates

Published by:
TRIDENT REFERENCE PUBLISHING
801 12th Avenue South, Suite 400
Naples, Fl 34102 USA

Tel: + 1 (239) 649-7077
www.tridentreference.com
email: sales@tridentreference.com

Party Plates
© TRIDENT REFERENCE PUBLISHING

Publisher
Simon St. John Bailey

Editor-in-chief
Susan Knightley

Prepress
Precision Prep & Press

Includes Index
ISBN 1582796599
UPC 6 15269 96599 3

Printed in The United States

introduction

Food, as grandmothers would say, appeals
first to the eyes. That's the point of parties:
to offer a variety of colorful, savory, tempting
dishes: food you can eat with your hands
along with drinks, wines or champagne.
A toast, an anniversary, a vernissage,
a celebration... many happy moments call

for a party. According to the time it will take place, serve appetizers or a complete meal; in this case, include nuts, sweets, liquors and coffee.

The presentation

It's best to present the bites in tiny portions, so they will be precisely that: bites, tidbits. To skillfully combine colors, flavors and textures of food should be the cook's prime objective.

Savory options

- Some simple and appealing ideas: Potato cakes topped with salmon, asparagus involtini with cured ham, mini cherry tomato brochettes, mozzarella bocconcini with basil, stuffed meat and rice olive leaves, skewers of oysters or mussels in pan-fried bacon-wraps, or sesame-seed-coated prawns marinated in soy sauce, or tiny onion and egg rolls, pink peppered quail eggs and mango cubes in skewers.

- These small delicacies can be served with cheese dips, tzatziki, mango sauce, soy sauce or watercress cream cheese.

Sweet options

- Chocolate covered walnuts, chocolate truffles and tiny meringues are tempting and easy to make.
- Fruit or cream sauce brochettes are fun to share in groups.
- Simple tidbits, like caramelized orange peels, Philadelphia-type cheese balls or mascarpone coated with chocolate seeds work as good complements at party endings, when serving coffee and the final toast.
- Crispy banana, sweet potato and apple chips, oven-dried in a low flame, go perfect with ice cream.

Difficulty scale

■☐☐I Easy to do

■■☐I Requires attention

■■■I Requires experience

tzatziki

■□□ | Cooking time: 0 minutes - Preparation time: 10 minutes

ingredients

> **1 large cucumber, peeled and grated**
> **500 g/1 lb natural yogurt**
> **1 tablespoon chopped fresh mint**
> **1 tablespoon chopped fresh parsley**
> **2 cloves garlic, crushed**
> **freshly ground black pepper**
> **2 French breadsticks**

method

1. Place cucumber, yogurt, mint, parsley, garlic and black pepper to taste in a bowl and mix to combine. Cover and refrigerate for at least 1 hour or until required.
2. To serve, accompany Tzatziki with broken or sliced bread for dipping.

....

Serves 8

tip from the chef

This easy dip makes a refreshing start to a meal and is also delicious served with raw vegetables. For a taste less acid than yogurt, use cottage cheese instead.

gado gado

■ ■ ☐ | Cooking time: 20 minutes - Preparation time: 35 minutes

method

1. To make sauce, heat oil in a frying pan over a medium heat, add onion and chili and cook, stirring, for 3 minutes or until onion is soft. Stir in peanut butter, coriander, coconut cream, kechap manis and chili sauce and stirring, bring to the boil. Reduce heat and simmer for 5 minutes, then stir in sugar and lemon juice. Cool slightly. The sauce should be slightly runny, if it is too thick add a little water.

2. Boil, steam or microwave beans and carrots, separately, until they are bright green and bright orange, then rinse under cold running water and drain well.

3. Heat oil in a frying pan or wok over a high heat, add tofu and stir-fry until golden. Drain on absorbent kitchen paper and cool slightly.

4. To serve, arrange piles of beans, carrots, tofu, red pepper, cucumbers, mushrooms and eggs on a large serving platter. Serve with sauce.

....

Serves 6

ingredients

> **125 g/4 oz green beans, sliced lengthwise**
> **2 carrots, cut into thick strips**
> **2 tablespoons vegetable oil**
> **185 g/6 oz firm tofu, cut into thick strips**
> **1 large red pepper, cut into thick strips**
> **2 cucumbers, cut into thick strips**
> **12 small button mushrooms**
> **6 hard-boiled eggs, cut into wedges**

peanut sauce

> **1 tablespoon peanut oil**
> **1 onion, finely chopped**
> **1 fresh red chili, finely chopped**
> **2/3 cup/170 g/5 1/2 oz peanut butter**
> **1 tablespoon ground coriander**
> **1/4 cup/185 ml/6 fl oz coconut cream**
> **3 tablespoons kechap manis**
> **2 teaspoons chili sauce**
> **1 teaspoon palm or brown sugar**
> **1 tablespoon lemon juice**

tip from the chef

Kechap manis is a thick sweet seasoning sauce used in Indonesian cooking. It is sometimes called Indonesian soy sauce. If unavailable, a mixture of soy sauce and dark corn syrup or golden syrup can be used in its place.

mango chicken bites

■ □ □ I Cooking time: 5 minutes - Preparation time: 10 minutes

ingredients

> **1 teaspoon ground cardamom**
> **2 teaspoons ground cumin**
> **¹/2 teaspoon chili powder**
> **1 teaspoon ground ginger**
> **5 boneless chicken breast fillets, cut into 2.5 cm/ 1 in pieces**
> **2 tablespoons oil**

mango sauce

> **1 cup/315 g/10 oz mango chutney**
> **¹/4 cup/60 ml/2 fl oz cream (double)**
> **1 tablespoon curry powder**

method

1. Place cardamom, cumin, chili powder and ginger in a bowl and mix to combine. Add chicken and toss to coat with spice mixture. Cover and set aside to marinate at room temperature for 1 hour.
2. Heat oil in a frying pan and cook chicken, stirring, over a medium heat for 5 minutes or until cooked. Remove from pan and drain on absorbent kitchen paper.
3. To make sauce, place chutney, cream and curry powder in a food processor or blender and process to combine. Serve as a dipping sauce with chicken.

Serves 20 as an hors d'œuvre

tip from the chef

As a starter for a formal meal you might like to arrange the chicken pieces on a bed of mixed lettuce leaves with slices of fresh or canned mango. The Mango Sauce could be served in individual pots on the side of each plate.

chicken cocktail
balls in plum sauce

■ ■ □ | Cooking time: 8 minutes - Preparation time: 35 minutes

method

1. In a food processor place all chicken ball ingredients except frying oil and process together quickly. With wetted hands shape into small balls. Place on a flat tray in a single layer and refrigerate for 30 minutes.

2. Heat oil, at least 5 cm deep in a frying pan, or half full in a deep fryer, to 180°C/350°F. Deep fry for about 3 to 4 minutes. Remove and drain on absorbent paper. Place a cocktail stick in each ball and arrange on platter.

3. To make sauce, place all ingredients in a small saucepan and bring slowly to the boil while stirring. Simmer for 2 minutes. Remove from heat and cool. Place dipping sauce in a bowl and serve with the chicken balls.

Serves 4

ingredients

> 500 g/1 lb ground chicken
> 10 shallots, finely chopped
> 1/4 teaspoon five spice powder
> 1 1/2 tablespoons honey
> 1 teaspoon lemon zest
> 2 tablespoons lemon juice
> 1 1/2 cups/90 g/3 oz fresh breadcrumbs
> oil for frying

plum sauce

> 1 cup/250 g/8 oz plum jam
> 1/2 cup/125 ml/4 fl oz white vinegar
> 1/4 teaspoon ground ginger
> 1/4 teaspoon ground allspice
> 1/8 teaspoon hot chili powder

tip from the chef

When accompanied by white rice, al dente, it makes for a complete meal. The rice makes a good match with the plum sauce, compensating the strong taste.

lemony
prawn kebabs

■ □ □ | Cooking time: 10 minutes - Preparation time: 20 minutes

ingredients

> **750 g/1¹/₂ lb large uncooked prawns, peeled and deveined**
> **16 button mushrooms, stalks removed**
> **2 green peppers, seeded and cut into 16 pieces**

marinade

> **60 ml/2 fl oz olive oil**
> **2 tablespoons lemon juice**
> **2 cloves garlic, crushed**
> **1 small red chili, seeded and finely chopped**
> **1 tablespoon chopped fresh sage**
> **freshly ground black pepper**

method

1. To make marinade, place oil, lemon juice, garlic, chili and sage in a bowl. Season to taste with black pepper and mix to combine. Add prawns and mushrooms and toss to coat with marinade. Set aside to marinate for 1 hour.

2. Thread prawns, mushrooms and green peppers alternately onto eight oiled wooden skewers. Grill kebabs for 8-10 minutes or until cooked, turning and basting with marinade during cooking.

....
Serves 4

tip from the chef
These are delightful on the barbecue.

oysters
marinated with bacon

■□□ | Cooking time: 5 minutes - Preparation time: 20 minutes

method

1. In a small bowl combine soy sauce, Worcestershire sauce, and honey. Set aside.
2. Wrap a bacon strip around each oyster, then thread two wrapped oysters on each skewer (you will need 12 small wooden sticks). Place skewers in a foil-lined grill pan. Pour marinade over oysters, cover and leave for 30 minutes.
3. Cook oysters under a preheated grill until bacon is golden. Serve immediately.

ingredients

> **2 tablespoons soy sauce**
> **1/2 teaspoon Worcestershire sauce**
> **1 tablespoon honey**
> **2 dozen oysters, shells discarded**
> **4 rashers rindless back bacon, cut into 3 cm/1 1/4 in long strips**

Makes **12**

tip from the chef

For a less greasy variation, wrap the oysters in slices of cured ham.

chicken
yakitori

■■□ | Cooking time: 5 minutes - Preparation time: 30 minutes

ingredients
> **400 g/14 oz chicken stir-fry**
> **1/2 cup/120 ml/4 fl oz soy sauce**
> **1/4 cup/60 g/2 fl oz honey**
> **1 clove garlic, crushed**
> **1/2 teaspoon ground ginger**

method
1. Place chicken in a glass bowl, mix in the soy sauce, honey, garlic and ginger (a). Cover, place in refrigerator and allow to marinate for several hours or overnight.
2. Thread chicken onto soaked small bamboo skewers, one or two strips each, using a weaving motion (b). Brush with marinade.
3. Heat grill or barbecue to high. Grease rack or plate with oil and arrange the skewers in a row (c). Cook for 2 1/2 minutes on each side, brush with marinade as they cook. Serve immediately.

Makes 25 small skewers

tip from the chef
For a change, make a tandoori sauce replacing the honey and soy sauce with a blended mixture of yogurt, garlic, onion, chili, ginger, coriander, salt, pepper and red food coloring.

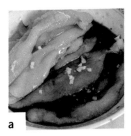
a

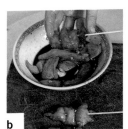
b

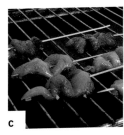
c

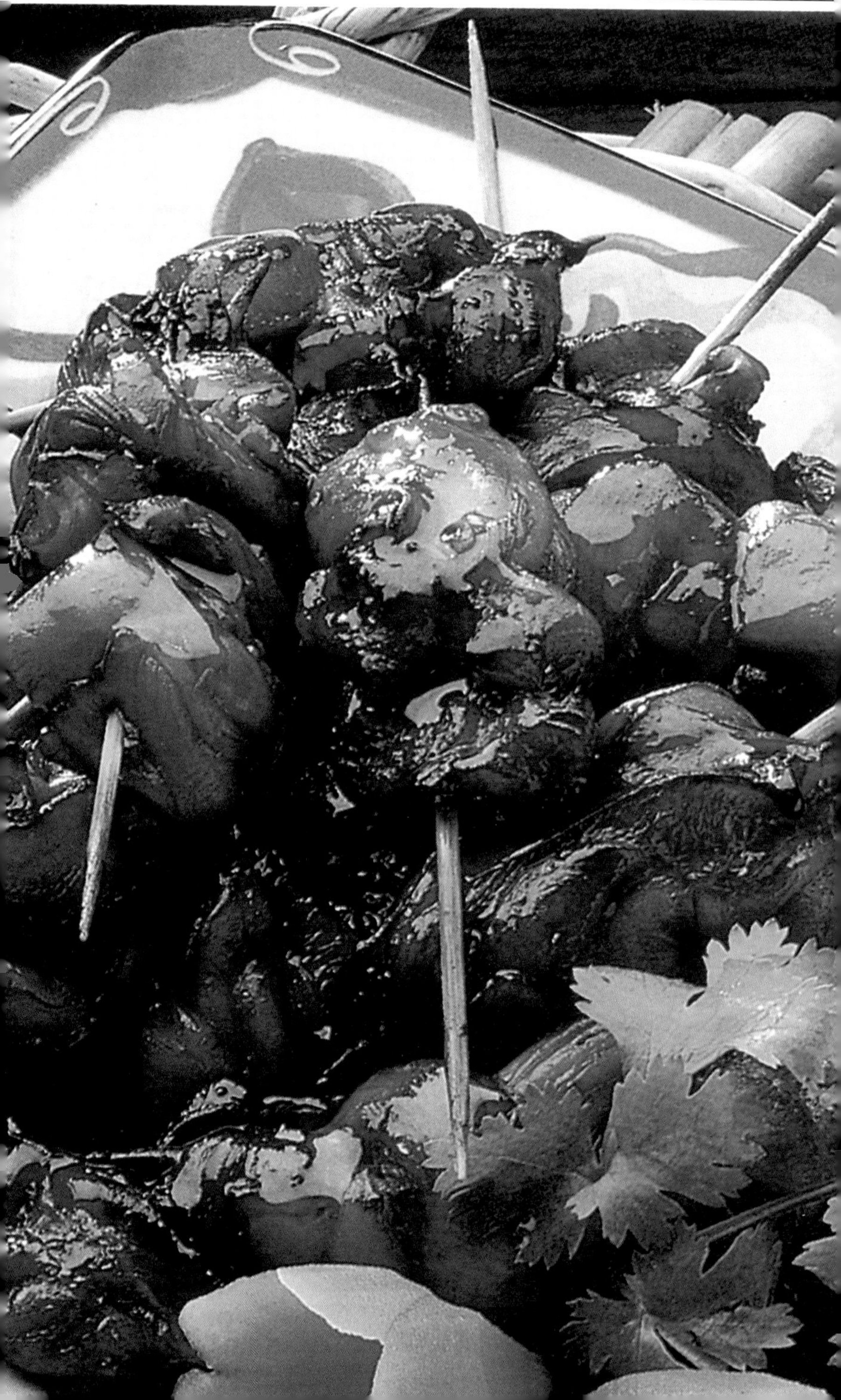

chicken
satay

■■□ | Cooking time: 5 minutes - Preparation time: 30 minutes

method

1. Combine water, peanut butter, honey, soy sauce, lemon juice, ginger and onion in a bowl. Stir in sambal oelek, if using, and mix well. Add chicken cubes, cover and marinate for at least 2 hours or overnight.
2. Soak cocktail sticks in cold water for 30 minutes, then drain. Remove chicken from marinade. Thread two pieces of chicken on each cocktail stick and set aside.
3. Pour marinade into a saucepan, bring to the boil, lower heat and simmer for about 10 minutes, or until sauce is reduced and thickened.
4. Cook chicken for about 10 minutes under a moderate grill or over hot coals, until tender. Serve four satay sticks per person, offering dipping sauce separately.

ingredients

> 125 ml/4 fl oz water
> 2 tablespoons smooth peanut butter
> 1 tablespoon honey
> 1 tablespoon light soy sauce
> 2 tablespoons lemon juice
> 1 teaspoon grated fresh ginger
> 1 onion, finely chopped
> 1 teaspoon sambal oelek or Tabasco sauce to taste, optional
> 500 g/1 lb chicken breast fillets, cut into 2 cm/3/4 in cubes

....
Serves 8

tip from the chef

You will need about 36 good-quality wooden cocktail sticks for this recipe.

bacon-wrapped
prawns

■□□ | Cooking time: 7 minutes - Preparation time: 20 minutes

method

1. To make marinade, place oregano, garlic, oil and vinegar in a bowl and whisk to combine. Add prawns and toss to coat. Cover and refrigerate for at least 1 hour or overnight.

2. Drain prawns and reserve marinade. Cut each bacon rasher into three pieces, wrap a piece of bacon around each prawn and secure with a wooden toothpick or cocktail stick.

3. Cook prawns under a preheated medium grill or on the barbecue, turning occasionally and brushing with reserved marinade, for 5 minutes or until bacon is crisp and prawns are cooked.

Makes about 24

ingredients

> **750 g/1½ lb large uncooked prawns, shelled and deveined, with tails left intact**
> **8 rashers bacon, rind removed**

herb marinade

> **2 tablespoons chopped fresh oregano**
> **2 cloves garlic, crushed**
> **½ cup/125 ml/4 fl oz olive oil**
> **2 tablespoons white wine vinegar**

tip from the chef

Prawns are delicious all by themselves. Another way to serve them is pan-fried in olive oil after sprinkling with lime juice and coating with a mixture of breadcrumbs and chopped parsley.

antipasto

■■□ | Cooking time: 30 minutes - Preparation time: 45 minutes

ingredients

> 1 large head cauliflower
> 750 g/1¹/₂ lb sweet pickled onions
> 4 stalks celery
> 2 medium zucchini
> 3 large green peppers
> 3 large red peppers
> 800 g/1³/₄ lb mushrooms
> 800 g/1³/₄ lb plum tomatoes
> 120 g/4 oz flat anchovy fillets
> 350 g/12¹/₂ oz canned flaked tuna
> 250 ml/9 fl oz vegetable oil
> 750 g/1¹/₂ lb stuffed green olives
> 400 g/14 oz kalamata olives
> 800 g/1³/₄ lb green beans
> 250 ml/9 fl oz tomato sauce
> 175 ml/6 fl oz chili sauce
> 125 ml/4¹/₂ fl oz white vinegar

method

1. Chop the cauliflower, onions, celery, zucchini, peppers, mushrooms and tomatoes. Drain the liquid from anchovies and tuna.
2. Rinse the anchovies and tuna under hot water. Chop the anchovies and break up the tuna.
3. Combine vegetable oil, cauliflower and onions in a large pan and cook over high heat for 10 minutes, stirring frequently. Add all other ingredients except the anchovies and tuna and vinegar and cook an additional 10 minutes, stirring frequently.
4. Add the anchovies, tuna and vinegar and cook another 10 minutes, stirring frequently. Set aside to cool.
5. Put the antipasto in sterilised jars and store in a refrigerator, it will keep for many weeks. Serve with cracker biscuits.

....
Makes enough for 20

tip from the chef
Serving this antipasto over little hot baguette slices enhances flavor and character.

carpaccio

■ ■ ☐ I Cooking time: 10 minutes - Preparation time: 50 minutes

method

1. Ask your butcher to cut the fillet into paper thin slices.
2. Cut breadstick into 1 cm/½ in slices, place in single layer on a baking tray, bake at 150°C/325°F/Gas 3 for 10 minutes or until bread is crisp but not dry; cool.
3. Spread thinly with combined butter, cheese and rind.
4. Place a slice of beef fillet onto each bread slice, top with a little tartare sauce, anchovy and capers, garnish with parsley.

Makes about 60

ingredients

> **500 g/1 lb piece beef eye fillet**
> **2 breadsticks**
> **90 g/3 oz butter**
> **2 tablespoons grated Parmesan cheese**
> **2 teaspoons grated lemon rind**
> **¹/₃ cup tartare sauce**
> **1 tablespoon chopped anchovy fillets**
> **2 tablespoons chopped capers**
> **parsley to garnish**

tip from the chef

Meats for carpaccio must be absolutely fresh, with no fat or nerves.

tuna
with wasabi butter

■□□ | Cooking time: 0 minutes - Preparation time: 25 minutes

ingredients

> **250 g/8 oz tuna steaks, cut 1 cm/1/2 in thick**
> **20 small rounds pumpernickel bread**

ginger marinade

> **2 teaspoons sesame oil**
> **1 tablespoon soy sauce**
> **1 clove garlic, crushed**
> **2 teaspoons grated fresh ginger**

wasabi butter

> **75 g/21/2 oz butter, softened**
> **1/2-1 teaspoon wasabi paste or wasabi powder mixed with water to form a paste**
> **2 tablespoons chopped fresh coriander**

method

1. To make marinade, place oil, soy sauce, garlic and ginger in a bowl and mix to combine. Cut tuna into thin slices. Add to marinade and toss to coat. Cover and set aside to marinate for 1 hour. Drain.

2. To make wasabi butter, place butter, wasabi paste and coriander in a small bowl and beat until smooth.

3. Spread pumpernickel rounds with wasabi butter, then top with tuna slices. Cover and chill until ready to serve.

....
Makes 20

tip from the chef
If fresh tuna is unavailable, use fresh salmon fillet.

curried
trim-lamb vol-au-vent

■ ■ □ | Cooking time: 22 minutes - Preparation time: 20 minutes

method

1. Heat nonstick pan over a high heat. Add lamb and fry for 2 minutes.
2. Add sauce, uncovered, for 10 minutes, stirring occasionally. Spoon into cases.
3. Preheat oven at 180°C/350°F/Gas 4 and cook vol-au-vent for 10 minutes. Serve hot, garnished with sprigs of coriander or a herb of choice.

ingredients

> **200 g/7 oz trim-lamb eye-of-loin or fillet, finely chopped**
> **³/4 cup prepared satay sauce**
> **2 x 60 g/2 oz packets vol-au-vent cases (total 24)**

Makes 24

tip from the chef
Rabbit, chicken or turkey are valid choices for stuffing these vol-au-vent.

baby *spinach tarts*

■■□ I Cooking time: 30 minutes - Preparation time: 40 minutes

ingredients

pastry

> 1^1/$_2$ cups/185 g/6 oz flour
> 4 tablespoons grated Parmesan cheese
> 100 g/3^1/$_2$ oz butter, chopped
> 2-3 tablespoons iced water

spinach filling

> 2 teaspoons olive oil
> 2 spring onions, chopped
> 1 clove garlic, crushed
> 8 spinach leaves, shredded
> 125 g/4 oz ricotta cheese, drained
> 2 eggs, lightly beaten
> ^{1}/$_3$ cup/90 ml/3 fl oz milk
> ^{1}/$_2$ teaspoon grated nutmeg
> 4 tablespoons pine nuts

method

1. To make pastry, place flour, cheese and butter (a) in a food processor and process until mixture resembles fine breadcrumbs.
2. With machine running, slowly add enough water to form a soft dough. Knead dough on a floured surface. Wrap in plastic food wrap (b) and refrigerate for 30 minutes.
3. Roll out pastry to 3 mm/^{1}/$_8$ in thick. Using an 8 cm/3^1/$_2$ in fluted pastry cutter, cut out twenty rounds. Place in lightly greased tins. Pierce base and sides with a fork and bake at 200°C/400°F/Gas 6 for 5-10 minutes.
4. To make filling, heat oil in a frying pan over a medium heat. Add spring onions, garlic and spinach and cook, stirring (c), until spinach is wilted. Remove pan from heat and set aside to cool.
5. Mix spinach mixture, ricotta cheese, eggs, milk and nutmeg (d) in a bowl. Spoon filling into pastry cases and sprinkle with pine nuts. Reduce oven temperature to 180°C/350°F/Gas 4 and bake for 15-20 minutes.

Makes 20

tip from the chef

These tiny tarts go well if pumpkin is used instead of spinach. To create a play of flavors and colors, serve both variations.

a

b

c

d

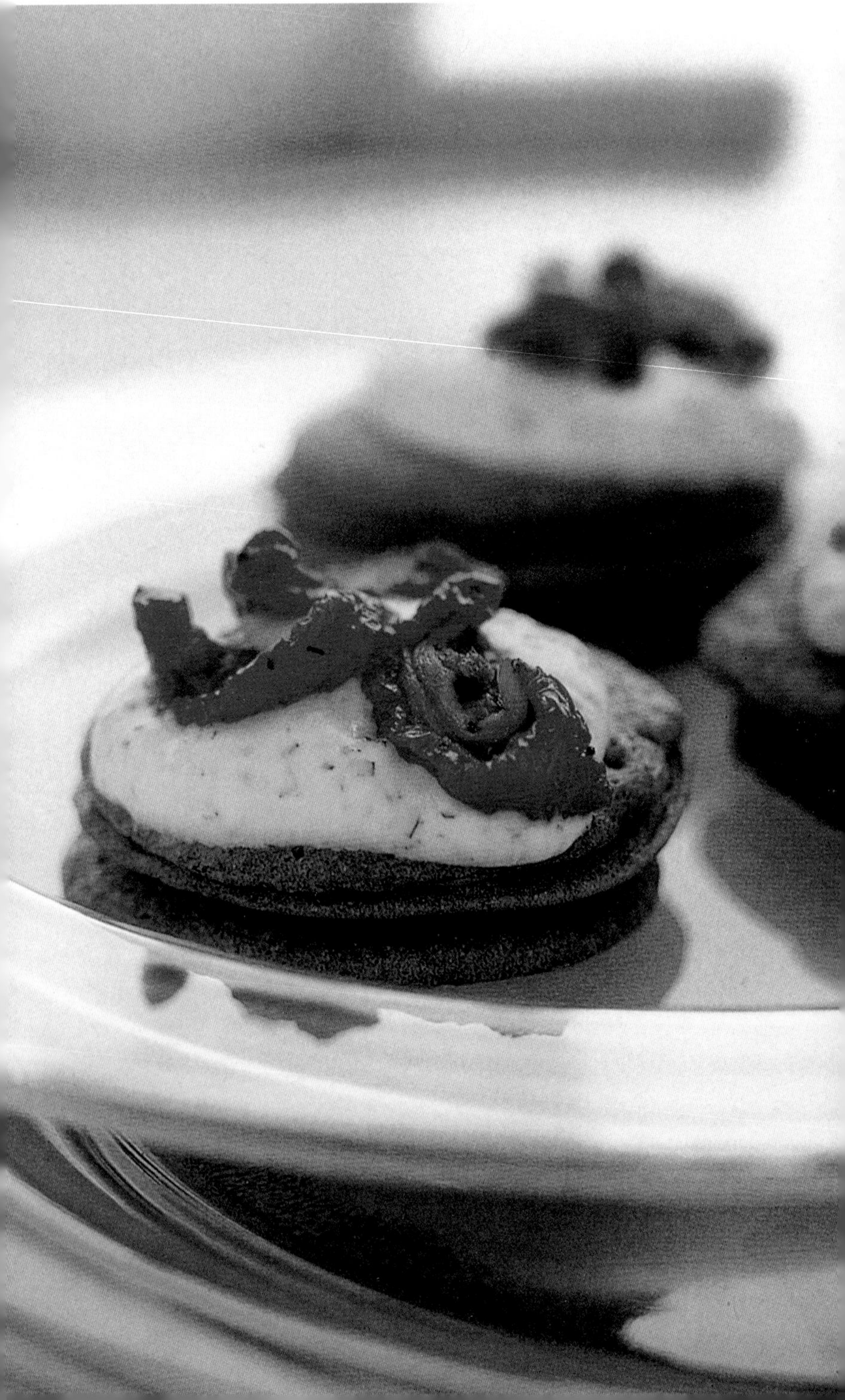

blini
with herbed yogurt

■ ■ □ | Cooking time: 10 minutes - Preparation time: 10 minutes

method

1. To make blini, place yeast, sugar and $^{1}/_{2}$ cup/125 ml/4fl oz of the milk in a small bowl. Stand for 5 minutes or until frothy.
2. Place buckwheat and plain flours in a large bowl. Mix to combine. Make a well in the center. Pour yeast mixture and remaining milk into well. Mix until just combined.
3. Place egg white in a separate clean bowl. Beat until soft peaks form. Fold egg mixture into batter. Season with black pepper to taste.
4. Heat a lightly oiled frying pan over a medium heat. Place tablespoons of mixture in pan. You should be able to cook 5-6 blini at a time in a 20-23 cm/8-10 in frying pan. Cook for 1-2 minutes or until bubbles appear on the surface. Turn over. Cook second side for 30 seconds until golden. Place on absorbent kitchen paper. Keep warm in a low oven while cooking the remaining mixture.
5. Serve blini warm or cold topped with a spoonful of yogurt. If desired add semi-dried tomatoes on top.

ingredients

> **200 g/7 oz natural yogurt, flavored with 1 tablespoon chopped fresh dill and 1 tablespoon chopped fresh mint**

blini

> 1 teaspoon dry yeast
> 1 teaspoon sugar
> 1$^{1}/_{2}$ cups/375 ml/ 12$^{1}/_{2}$ fl oz milk, warmed
> $^{1}/_{2}$ cup/130 g/4 oz buckwheat flour
> $^{1}/_{2}$ cup/125 g/4 oz plain flour
> 1 egg white
> freshly ground black pepper

....
Makes 20

tip from the chef

For a delicious sweet version, add 2 tablespoons sugar to batter. And instead of yogurt, use ganache (a half-and-half mix of cream and chocolate melted over a low heat).

marinated
mushrooms

a

■□□ | Cooking time: 0 minutes - Preparation time: 25 minutes

method

1. Trim stalks from mushrooms (a) and wipe with a clean damp teatowel. Place mushrooms in a bowl, pour over boiling water (b) and lemon juice and stand for 5 minutes.
2. To make marinade, place parsley, thyme, garlic, oil, vinegar and black pepper to taste in a screwtop jar or in a bowl (c) and shake to combine.
3. Drain mushrooms, return to bowl, pour over marinade (d), cover and marinate in the refrigerator for at least 2 hours or overnight.

Makes about 30

ingredients

> 500 g/1 lb button mushrooms
> 1 cup/250 ml/8 fl oz boiling water
> 2 tablespoons lemon juice

mushroom marinade

> 1 tablespoon chopped fresh parsley
> 2 teaspoons chopped fresh thyme
> 2 cloves garlic, crushed
> 1/3 cup/90 ml/3 fl oz olive oil
> 2 tablespoons white wine vinegar
> freshly ground black pepper

tip from the chef

To add an exotic touch to the delicate flavor of mushrooms, it's good to use a mixture of pink, green and Sechuan pepper instead of the black.

b

c

d

celery boats

■□□ I Cooking time: 0 minutes - Preparation time: 30 minutes

ingredients

> **6 stalks celery**
> **375 g/12 oz medium shrimps, cooked**
> **1 tablespoon red lumpfish roe**
> **1 tablespoon snipped fresh chives**

chive and caper filling

> **1 tablespoon snipped fresh chives**
> **1 tablespoon chopped capers**
> **1 tablespoon Dijon mustard**
> **1¹/4 cups/315 g /10 oz sour cream**

method

1. To make filling, place chives, capers, mustard and sour cream in a bowl and mix to combine. Cover and refrigerate until required.

2. Trim and cut celery into 5 cm/2 in long pieces. Spoon or pipe filling into celery boats. Top each boat with a shrimp and garnish with lumpfish roe and chives.

....
Makes about 24

tip from the chef
Celery stalks, perfect for making morsels, can also be used as improvised spoons for dips and other soft preparations.

herb-filled
cherry tomatoes

■ ■ □ | Cooking time: 0 minutes - Preparation time: 45 minutes

method

1. Cut tops off tomatoes and carefully scoop out seeds. Reserve 2 tablespoons of the pulp (a). Place tomatoes up side down on absorbent kitchen paper and drain.
2. To make filling, place cream cheese in a food processor and process until light and fluffy. Add reserved tomato pulp, mint, parsley, chives, almonds and black pepper to taste (b) and process briefly to combine.
3. Spoon or pipe filling into tomato shells (c) and arrange on a serving platter. Cover and refrigerate for 1 hour or until firm.

Makes about 36

ingredients

> 500 g/1 lb cherry tomatoes

herb cheese filling

> 125 g/4 oz cream cheese, softened
> 1 tablespoon chopped fresh mint
> 1 tablespoon chopped fresh parsley
> 1 tablespoon snipped fresh chives
> 45 g/1 1/2 oz slivered almonds, toasted
> freshly ground black pepper

tip from the chef

A simple and quick stuffing for cherry tomatoes: drained canned tuna blended with cream cheese and capers.

a

b

c

potato-smoked
salmon bites

■□□ I Cooking time: 45 minutes - Preparation time: 15 minutes

method

1. Wash potatoes, cut in half and place cut side down. Scoop out a cavity in the top.
2. Toss in oil, then place cut side down on oven tray and bake at 180°C/350°/Gas 4 for 45 minutes or until tender. Allow to cool slightly.
3. Place some salmon in each cavity, followed by a spoonful of sour cream over each. Top with a wedge of egg, then garnish with dill.

ingredients

> **16 small pontiac potatoes**
> **¼ cup/60 ml/2 fl oz oil**
> **250 g/½ lb smoked salmon**
> **½ cup/120 ml/4 fl oz sour cream**
> **3 hard-boiled eggs, sliced**
> **fresh dill for garnish**

Makes 32

tip from the chef

The combination of potatoes, smoked salmon, cheese, dill and eggs is simply perfect, and fully Scandinavian. Excellent with champagne or a white California varietal wine.

prosciutto-wrapped
asparagus

■□□ | Cooking time: 7 minutes - Preparation time: 15 minutes

method

1. Boil, steam or microwave asparagus until just tender. Drain and rinse under cold running water until cool. Drain asparagus again and dry on absorbent kitchen paper.
2. Cut each slice of prosciutto or ham lengthwise into 3 long strips and wrap each strip around an asparagus spear. Cover and refrigerate until required.

ingredients

> **250 g/8 oz fresh asparagus spears, trimmed**
> **4 slices prosciutto or lean ham**

Makes about 12

tip from the chef

For the asparagus to be tender as well as firm, cooking must be watchful. If cooked in asparagus boiler, place the shoots pointing up so they are not in contact with the water.

prosciutto
melon

■☐☐ | Cooking time: 0 minutes - Preparation time: 15 minutes

ingredients
> **1 cantaloupe melon**
> **250 g/8 oz very thinly sliced prosciutto or lean ham**

method
1. Cut melon in half lengthwise and scoop out seeds. Cut each half into 8 wedges, remove skin and cut in half, crosswise.
2. Cut each slice of prosciutto or ham lengthwise into 3 strips and wrap one strip around each piece of melon. Arrange on a serving plate, cover and chill.

....
Makes 32

tip from the chef
This is an overly classic match. For an original variation, replace melon for mango, papaya or avocado.

spiced
almonds and pecans

■ □ □ | Cooking time: 8 minutes - Preparation time: 5 minutes

method

1. Heat oil in a frying pan over a medium heat, add almonds, pecans and sugar and cook, stirring, until nuts are golden. Transfer to a heatproof bowl.
2. Combine cumin, salt and chili powder, sprinkle over hot nuts and toss to coat. Cool for 5 minutes, then serve.

Makes 2¹/2 cups/350 g/11 oz

ingredients

> ¹/4 cup/60 ml/2 fl oz peanut oil
> **220 g/7 oz whole blanched almonds**
> **125 g/4 oz whole pecans**
> ¹/4 cup/60 g/2 oz sugar
> **2 teaspoons ground cumin**
> **1 teaspoon salt**
> **1 teaspoon chili powder**

tip from the chef

For this recipe use any type of walnuts, as well as chestnuts, previously boiled and peeled.

apricots with
blue-cheese topping

■□□ | Cooking time: 1 minute - Preparation time: 5 minutes

ingredients
> **12 fresh apricots or 850 g/28 oz canned apricot halves**
> **250 g/1/2 lb soft blue cheese**

method
1. Cut apricots in half and remove seed (or drain canned apricots well on absorbent paper).
2. Place apricots cut side up on serving plate and spread each with a teaspoon of cheese.
3. If desired, apricots and cheese may be grilled for about 1 minute or until cheese begins to melt. Serve immediately.

....

Makes 24

tip from the chef
The remotely sweet flavor of apricots matches well with cheeses as camembert, crottin (of goat) or feta (of sheep).

crocked
cheese

■□□ I Cooking time: 0 minutes - Preparation time: 5 minutes

method

1. Combine all ingredients in a food processor. Blend well. Turn the mixture into a crock or serving bowl. Sprinkle additional poppy seeds on top for garnish.
2. Refrigerate until ready to serve. Serve with an assortment of crackers.

Makes about 1^1/$_3$ cups/360 g/12 oz

ingredients

> ^{1}/$_2$ cup/60 g/2 oz cottage cheese
> ^{1}/$_2$ cup/60 g/2 oz ricotta cheese
> ^{1}/$_2$ cup/60 g/2 oz grated Cheddar cheese
> 65g/2 oz butter
> ^{1}/$_2$ cup/30 g/1 oz shallots, chopped
> 30 ml/1 fl oz beer
> 1 teaspoon Dijon mustard
> 1 teaspoon paprika
> ^{1}/$_4$ teaspoon salt
> 1-2 teaspoons poppy seeds

tip from the chef

Mustard and paprika are not indispensable, and can be used alternatively.

cheese
and chive croquettes

■■□ | Cooking time: 5 minutes - Preparation time: 45 minutes

ingredients

> **500 g/1 lb grated mozzarella cheese**
> **1¹/₂ cups/185 g/6 oz flour**
> **4 tablespoons snipped fresh chives**
> **¹/₂ teaspoon cayenne pepper**
> **2 eggs, lightly beaten**
> **¹/₂ cup/60 g/2 oz cornflour**
> **vegetable oil for deep-frying**

method

1. Place mozzarella cheese, 1 cup/125 g/4 oz flour, chives, cayenne pepper and eggs in a bowl (a) and mix to combine. Shape mixture into balls, place on a plate lined with plastic food wrap and refrigerate for 30 minutes.

2. Combine cornflour and remaining flour on a plate. Roll balls in flour mixture (b) and chill for 10 minutes.

3. Heat oil in a saucepan until a cube of bread dropped in browns in 50 seconds. Deep-fry croquettes, in batches (c), for 4-5 minutes or until golden. Drain on absorbent kitchen paper and serve.

....
Makes 24

tip from the chef
These delicious cheese puffs can be made with finely chopped spring onions.

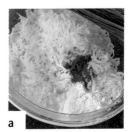

a

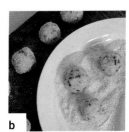

b

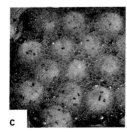

c

devilled eggs

■ ■ □ | Cooking time: 10 minutes - Preparation time: 30 minutes

method

1. Place eggs in a saucepan, cover with cold water and bring to the boil. Stirring gently will keep the yolks centered. Discontinue stirring, reduce heat and simmer for 10 minutes. Drain eggs, then rinse under cold running water until cool enough to handle.

2. Peel eggs and cut in half lengthwise. Remove yolks and place in a bowl. Set whites aside. Add mustard, curry powder, mayonnaise and cream and mash until mixture is well combined and smooth.

3. Spoon egg yolk mixture into a piping bag fitted with a small star nozzle and pipe rosettes into reserved egg white shells. Garnish with chives or dill.

ingredients

> **12 eggs**
> **1 teaspoon dry mustard**
> **1 teaspoon curry powder**
> **2 tablespoons mayonnaise**
> **2 tablespoons thickened (double) cream**
> **snipped fresh chives or dill**

Makes 24

tip from the chef

For hard-boiled eggs to come out perfect, they must be at room temperature before cooking. Boil 10 minutes, no longer, so that egg whites are not gummy; then leave 7-8 minutes in cold water to peel easily.

chocolate
macadamia clusters

■□□ I Cooking time: 5 minutes - Preparation time: 25 minutes

ingredients
> **300 g/10 oz dark chocolate, chopped**
> **200 g/7 oz roasted macadamia nuts**
> **1/2 cup/45 g/11/2 oz shredded coconut**

method
1. Melt chocolate in a bowl over a saucepan of simmering water.
2. Chop macadamia nuts into chunks.
3. Add nuts and shredded coconut to chocolate, stir to coat.
4. Place heaped teaspoonfuls of mixture onto foil-lined tray, allow to set.

....
Makes about 24

tip from the chef
Chocolate topping can also be made over caramelized orange peels or pecan nuts.

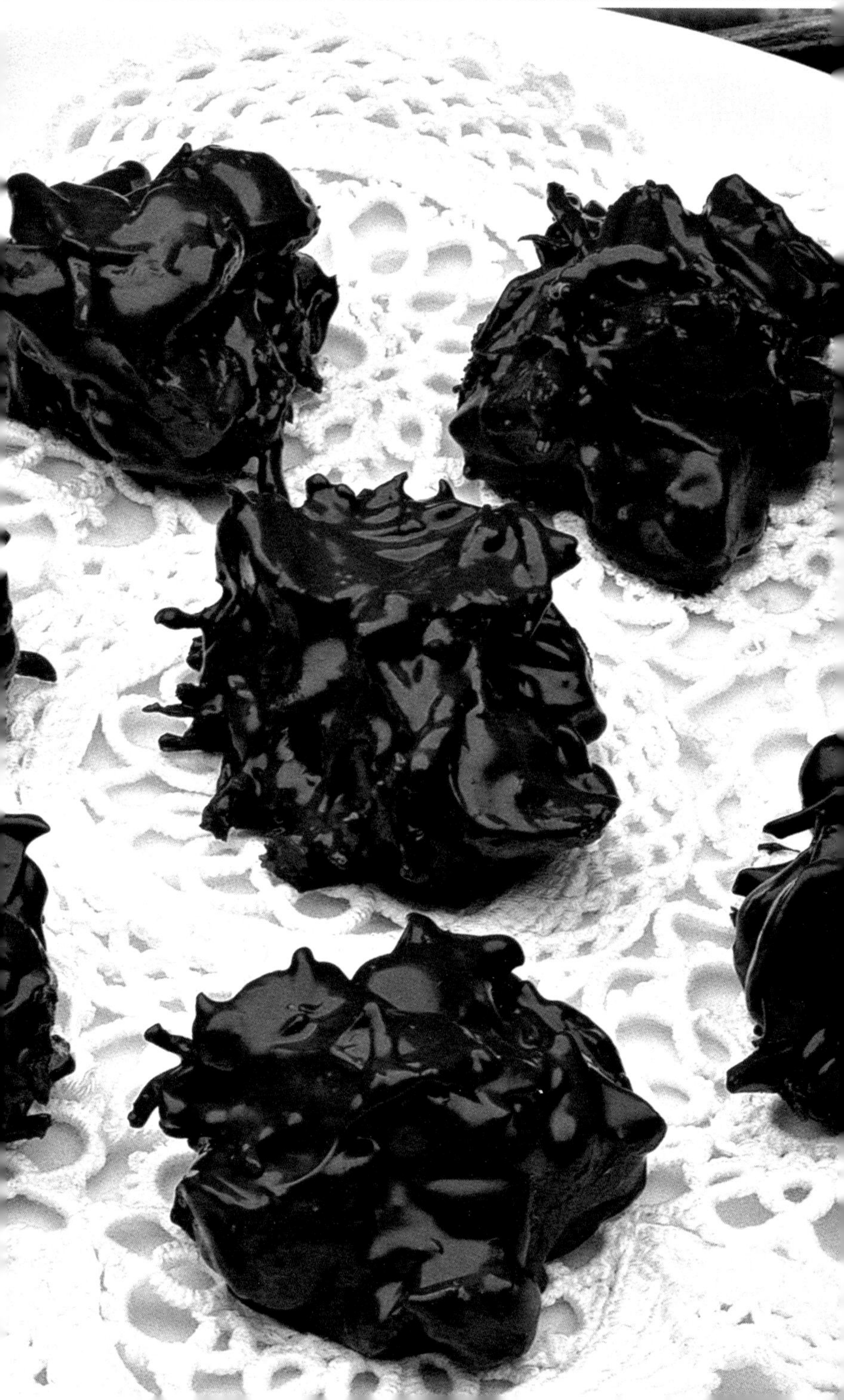

fruit kebabs

■□□ | Cooking time: 0 minutes - Preparation time: 30 minutes

method

1. To make sauce, place mint, honey, sour cream and cream in a bowl and mix to combine. Cover and refrigerate until ready to serve.
2. Peel melon, remove seeds and cut into bite-size pieces. Cut kiwi fruit in half. Thread two pieces of fruit onto each stick (you will need 16 wooden cocktail sticks). Serve with the sauce.

....

Makes 16

ingredients

> 1 small cantaloupe melon
> 4 kiwi fruit, peeled and quartered
> 250 g/8 oz strawberries, hulled
> 16 wooden cocktail sticks

honey cream sauce

> 2 tablespoons chopped fresh mint
> 2 tablespoons honey
> 1 cup/250 g/8 oz sour cream
> 1 cup/250 ml/8 fl oz cream (double)

tip from the chef

Fruit brochettes, fully summery, can be a great ending for a party or a meritorious dessert at an informal dinner with friends.

coffee meringues

a

■ ■ □ | Cooking time: 60 minutes - Preparation time: 30 minutes

method

1. Place sugar and water in a small saucepan, over a medium heat, stirring (a) until sugar dissolves. Bring to the boil and boil for 1-2 minutes. Brush any sugar grains from sides of pan with a wet pastry brush.

2. Beat egg white until stiff peaks form. Continue beating while pouring in hot syrup in a thin stream (b), a little at a time. Beat until meringue is thick. Fold in vinegar, cornflour (c) and coffee essence.

3. Place mixture in a large piping bag fitted with a fluted tube. Pipe 4 cm/1³/4 in stars (d) onto greased and lined oven trays. Bake at 140°C/280°F/Gas 2 for 1 hour or until firm and dry. Cool in oven with door ajar.

ingredients

> ³/4 cup/185 g raw sugar
> 3 tablespoons water
> 1 egg white
> 1 teaspoon white vinegar
> 2 teaspoons cornflour
> 2 teaspoons coffee essence

....
Makes 30

tip from the chef

Who would believe that these delicious morsels are free of fat and cholesterol? They are perfect to serve with coffee or as an afternoon tea treat.

b

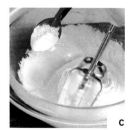
c

d

index